Palm Springs

WINTER
GOLF CAPITAL
OF THE WORLD

Palm Springs
HOLIDAY

A Vintage Tour from Palm Springs to the Salton Sea

PETER MORUZZI

GIBBS SMITH
TO ENRICH AND INSPIRE HUMANKIND
Salt Lake City | Charleston | Santa Fe | Santa Barbara

First Edition
15 14   7 8 9

All images from author's collection except for the following:
Daniel M. Callahan: 134 (left, right), 135–137, 138 (bottom),
139–146; Coachella Valley Historical Society: 10, 156 (left, top
right), 157, 158 (left), 161–162, 164; Bruce Emerton: 24 (bottom
left, bottom right), 25 (top left), 32 and 33 (background), 35
(bottom), 37 (top left), 42, 46 (right), 54, 56 (top right, bottom
right), 57, 60 (top left), 65, 79 (bottom left), 84 (bottom right), 85
(top), 92 (top, top left, bottom left), 93, 98 (bottom), 99, 110 (top),
124 (left), 128 (left), 152 (bottom left), 156 (bottom right), 165
(top left); Kiara Geller: 119 (bottom middle, bottom right); Scott
Kennedy: 46 (bottom), 67 (top right), 77 (top right, bottom right),
79 (top right), 88 (top right), 97 (bottom right), 119 (top), 120–121,
128 (bottom right); Palm Desert Historical Society: 13 (top right),
30 (top right, bottom right), 62 (top right), 147 (top), 149; Palm
Springs Historical Society: 11, 20 (left), 25 (right), 29, 38 and 39
(background), 41, 43, 59, 68 (left), 130; Doug Park: author photo

Published by
Gibbs Smith
P.O. Box 667
Layton, Utah 84041

Orders: 1.800.835.4993
www.gibbs-smith.com

Designed by Kurt Wahlner
Printed and bound in China
Gibbs Smith books are printed on either recycled, 100% post-
consumer waste, FSC-certified papers or on paper produced from a
100% certified sustainable forest/controlled wood source.

Library of Congress Cataloging-in-Publication Data

Moruzzi, Peter.
  Palm Springs holiday : a vintage tour from Palm Springs to the Salton Sea
/ Peter Moruzzi. — 1st ed.
      p. cm.
  ISBN-13: 978-1-4236-0476-1
  ISBN-10: 1-4236-0476-8
  1. Palm Springs (Calif.)—History—Pictorial works. 2. Palm Springs
(Calif.)—Social life and customs—Pictorial works. 3. Historic buildings—
California—Palm Springs—Pictorial works. 4. Palm Springs (Calif.)—
Buildings, structures, etc.—Pictorial works. 5. Palm Springs Region
(Calif.)—History—Pictorial works. 6. Coachella Valley (Calif.)—History—
Pictorial works. I. Title.
  F869.P18M476 2009
  979.4'97—dc22
                                                2009000539

Contents

Acknowledgments

Among the many friends who assisted in the realization of *Palm Springs Holiday,* it is Jeffrey Komori—my coproducer and the technical wizard behind the original documentary *Desert Holiday,* upon which this book is based—to whom I am most indebted. Thanks also to Daniel M. Callahan, Connie Cowan, Bruce Emerton, Kiara Geller, Scott Kennedy, Sven A. Kirsten, Lydia Kremer, Nickie McLaughlin, Sally McManus, Tony Merchell, Karen Prinzmetal, Hal Rover, Jeri Vogelsang, and Jim West for their valuable assistance. I am grateful for having had access to the rich archives of the Coachella Valley Historical Society, Palm Desert Historical Society, Palm Springs Historical Society, and the Palm Springs Public Library. And it is with heartfelt thanks that I acknowledge my editor, Jared Smith, and my ever-enthusiastic publisher, Gibbs Smith, whose open mind and *joie de vivre* remains an inspiration. Finally, my highest praise goes to book designer Kurt Wahlner, whose affection for the subject resulted in a better book than I ever envisioned.

This is the story of the Coachella Valley—home of Palm Springs, Rancho Mirage, Palm Desert, La Quinta, Indio, and other desert cities—as experienced by the average tourist who vacationed here from the 1910s through the 1960s. It is the story of a Palm Springs holiday that you or I might have once taken to "America's Foremost Desert Resort."

Many of the images in this book are picture postcards and brochures obtained at gift shops or picked up at

Introduction

hotels, inns, restaurants, nightclubs, and the many attractions available in this desert playground during the last century.

Postcards are unique because, as historical records, they represent an idealized world of captured moments staged like movie publicity shots. Postcards are also a not-so-subtle way of letting someone who's freezing in Cleveland know that you're enjoying 80 degree temperatures, boundless sunshine, and endless nights of dining, drinking, and dancing in the desert. So come along, put on your sunwear and hop into your motorcar for a road trip through this desert wonderland.

Early History

For hundreds of years prior to the arrival of white settlers, the desert, rivers, canyons, sand dunes, alluvial fans, and soaring mountains of the Coachella Valley were the home of native hunter-gatherers called the Cahuilla. Those who resided in the western end of the valley, where Palm Springs is today, became known as the Agua Caliente Band of Cahuilla Indians for their association with the area's natural mineral hot springs.

BACKGROUND: Driving past blooming desert verbena after winter rains, 1927. LEFT: Members of Palm Springs' Agua Caliente Band of Cahuilla Indians.

ABOVE: Tahquitz Falls; LEFT: Mount San Jacinto, as seen from the desert floor.

Following the discovery of gold near Sacramento in 1849 and the arrival of the transcontinental railroad through the Coachella Valley in 1875, interest in the desert began to germinate. In remunerating the Southern Pacific Railroad for linking the North American coasts, Congress awarded the company a checkerboard gift of land consisting of every other section (one square mile) for ten miles on either side of its tracks. In the Coachella Valley, the remaining sections of "worthless" desert land were eventually given to the local Indian tribes to serve as reservations— sovereign nations of alternating desert squares. Unbeknownst to Congress or the railroad, natural mineral hot springs located at the base of Mount San Jacinto would be one of the magnets that attracted people to the area in later years.

Upper Palm Canyon.

William Pester, the original Palm Springs "nature boy," in Palm Canyon with his guitar, circa 1917.

*I*n the early 1910s, Palm Springs was still mostly agricultural, with open grazing land, orchards, and farm animals. A large irrigation ditch, called a *zanja*, was dug to provide water to the area from the nearby Whitewater River.

A *zanja* brings water to Palm Springs from the Whitewater River.

Native *Washingtonia filifera* palms, with Palm Springs in the background, circa 1910.

AGUA CALIENTE BATH HOUSE, PALM SPRINGS, CAL.

Another attraction was the soon-discovered benefit of dry, warm air—particularly during winter months—to tubercular patients from back east. Then, in the early twentieth century, the area's close proximity to the booming metropolis of Los Angeles proved to be Palm Springs' greatest asset.

By this time, the Agua Caliente Band of Cahuilla Indians, who cherished their hot springs, had constructed a modest bathhouse for locals and visitors, accommodating up to four bathers.

ABOVE: The Agua Caliente Indians' original bathhouse; LEFT: Looking north on Indian Avenue (now Indian Canyon Drive), circa 1919.

Palm Springs, California and Mt. San Jacinto as seen from the Air

OB-H906

The village of Palm Springs sits at the foot of majestic Mount San Jacinto, as seen from the air, 1940.

In 1959, the baths would become the site of the ultramodern Spa Bathhouse and Hotel—the tribe's first major investment, which set the stage for their massive casino resorts of recent years.

Finally, with the advent of motion pictures, Palm Springs became a convenient retreat for the entertainment industry and, soon, wealthy industrialists from the East and Midwest.

Along with the health seekers, celebrities, and moneyed elite came ordinary middle-class Americans who were just as eager to bask in the warm winter sun.

The Original Hotels

The embrace of Palm Springs by winter sunseekers following World War I led to the opening of numerous hotels at the foot of Mount San Jacinto.

LEFT: The entrance to the Desert Inn, circa 1928; BACKGROUND: The Oasis Hotel, circa 1925.

Palm Springs Hotel

The first hotel erected in the Coachella Valley was Dr. Welwood Murray's Palm Springs Hotel, with accommodations for twenty guests. It opened in 1887. Author Robert Louis Stevenson and naturalist John Muir were two notable visitors to Murray's small hotel.

La Palma Hotel

Another early lodging was Otto Adler's La Palma Hotel, located on what became Palm Canyon Drive. But Adler was not the visionary who would make Palm Springs what it was destined to become.

ABOVE: Dr. Welwood Murray, the village's first hotel keeper, stands in front of the gate of his Palm Springs hotel; RIGHT: Otto Adler rustles up some vittles for his guests.

Desert Inn

In 1909, scrappy pioneer settlers Dr. Harry and Nellie Coffman purchased a modest cluster of shacks and canvas tents that already served as a sanitarium for tuberculosis sufferers. They renamed the property the Desert Inn and Sanitorium. In 1917, following the departure of Dr. Coffman for Calexico, Nellie dropped sanitorium from the hotel's name and, with her two sons, George Roberson and Earl Coffman, erected a large main building as the Desert Inn's new centerpiece.

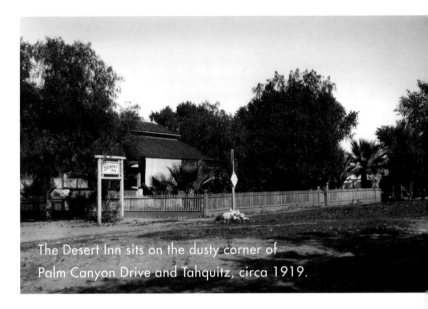

The Desert Inn sits on the dusty corner of Palm Canyon Drive and Tahquitz, circa 1919.

Relaxing under the ramada was part of the Desert Inn experience in 1918.

Believing that the future of Palm Springs was not as a health retreat but as a winter resort, the farsighted Nellie Coffman and her boys set about creating a place of rest and privacy of ever-increasing luxury. Over the next forty years, Nellie Coffman made the Desert Inn arguably the most famous desert resort in America.

LEFT: Nellie Coffman, grand dame of Palm Springs, and her two sons, George Roberson (left) and Earl Coffman, 1926; BELOW: Décor was rustic Spanish at the Desert Inn, where the western theme was taking root.

LEFT: Barefoot and shirtless, hermit Edward Fitzgerald poses for a publicity shot.

By the 1940s, the Desert Inn had become so famous that even Edward Fitzgerald, another Palm Springs hermit, couldn't resist posing in front of its famous entry gates.

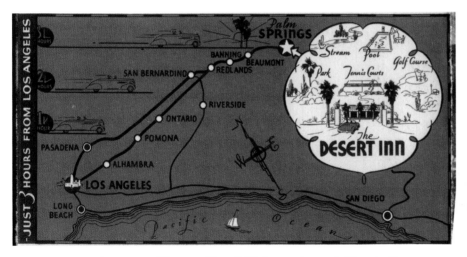

From Los Angeles, it was only three hours by motorcar and you were in Palm Springs.

From the Midwest and East, the Southern Pacific Railroad's *Sunset Limited* stopped at Palm Springs' Spanish-style train station north of the village.

S·P

the friendly Southern Pacific

Cowboys have been part of the Coachella Valley scene for much of the twentieth century. Here, a singing cowboy croons for the kiddies, including a young Shirley Temple (on right).

Oasis Hotel

ABOVE: The Oasis Hotel with its dramatic bell tower made a strong architectural statement in sleepy Palm Springs; BELOW: The Oasis Hotel's interior courtyard.

Another important early resort was Pearl McManus's Oasis Hotel, designed in 1923 by Lloyd Wright, the talented architect son of Frank Lloyd Wright.

Constructed of slip-form concrete in a style unique to Lloyd Wright, the Oasis Hotel is architecturally significant because it was one of the earliest Modern hotels built in Southern California.

Hotel The Oasis, Palm Springs, California

A cluster of desert modern buildings are added to the Oasis Hotel property in the 1950s; architect E. Stewart Williams was also responsible for the two-story Oasis Building erected in 1952. Its major tenant was the Milton F. Kreis drugstore.

The Oasis HOTEL

PALM SPRINGS, CALIF.

During World War II, perhaps to camouflage it from enemy bombers, the Oasis Hotel was covered entirely by vines.

In the early 1950s, local architect E. Stewart Williams designed a large addition to the hotel with a cluster of stylish Modern buildings on the west side of the street.

The new Oasis commercial building took over a large portion of the old Oasis Hotel property.

Scene on South Palm Canyon Drive, Palm Springs, California

Palm Springs

California

Pearl McCallum McManus in 1955.

El Mirador Resort

At the tail end of the madcap 1920s, entrepreneur P. T. Stevens opened the fabulous El Mirador Hotel just in time for the 1929 stock market crash. Going far beyond any Palm Springs hotel existing at that time in size and amenities, the El Mirador included a huge swimming pool, a golf course, a nightclub, and a spa. In fact, the first golf course in the Coachella Valley was at the El Mirador.

The 1929 opening of the fabulous El Mirador Hotel.

Nonetheless, the hotel barely survived the Great Depression and subsequent conversion into the U.S. Army's Torney General Hospital during World War II.

The El Mirador's vast grounds included an Olympic-size swimming pool and a golf course.

Swimming Pool in Patio of
Hotel Del Tahquitz
Palm Springs, California

Hotel Del Tahquitz
Palm Springs, California

Del Tahquitz Hotel

Despite the Great Depression, people with money continued to visit Palm Springs during the 1930s. Hotels such as the Pueblo Revival–style Del Tahquitz served the growing demand for accommodations.

Once located on the south end of downtown Palm Springs, the Del Tahquitz received a Spanish makeover in the 1940s.

Kicking up their heels at the Del Tahquitz.

Racquet Club

In 1936, motion picture stars Charlie Farrell and Ralph Bellamy opened the Racquet Club resort—including tennis courts, cocktail lounge, Bamboo Room nightclub, and bungalows—that was very popular with the Hollywood crowd.

Marilyn Monroe was supposedly discovered here while lounging around the pool. Farrell later became mayor of Palm Springs.

Just east of Palm Springs, the army conducted desert training exercises under the command of General George Patton in preparation for the Allied invasion of North Africa.

ABOVE: General Patton (center) surveys the mock battleground with his officers in 1942; BELOW: Army tanks parked near Palm Springs await action in North Africa.

FACING: Good ol' Charlie even let some of his fancier guests park their 1956 Cadillacs poolside at the Racquet Club.

GROVE BLDG.

Arrival of the Spanish Style

The majority of pre–World War II tourist accommodations in Palm Springs were inspired by the Spanish Colonial Revival style that was popular in Southern California during the 1920s and 1930s. At the time, the Spanish style was felt to be the most responsive to California's history and climate. Typical examples include the Royal Palms Hotel and the El Patio Court.

FACING: The Royal Palms Hotel was a typical Spanish-style resort; LEFT: It's almost siesta time on quiet Palm Canyon Drive.

Depression-era cars parked in front of the Hotel Bella Vista.

BELOW: At the Monte Vista Hotel and Apartments, life was as simple as a friendly game of cards played on a patchwork of colored squares.

MONTE VISTA HOTEL & APTS.
414 No. Palm Canyon Drive
Palm Springs, Calif.

THE MIRA MONTE, PALM SPRINGS, CALIFORNIA

The Wigwam
Palm Springs, Calif.

ABOVE: The Mira Monte Hotel and Apartments in the 1930s; LEFT: Where's the wigwam at the Wigwam?

The wonderful Spanish Colonial Revival–style La Plaza shopping center opened in 1936, designed by Harry Williams, the father of renowned Palm Springs Desert Modern architect E. Stewart Williams. Current research by architectural historian Alan Hess indicates that La Plaza, with its broad mix of retail stores, was perhaps the first true automobile-oriented shopping center in California.

Looking south down Palm Canyon Drive in the 1930s (above) and later in 1941 (above right).

A "Lazy Person's Postcard" from 1939.

Palm Springs, California   Date...................

DEAR					Salton Sea
Mother	Dad				Painted Canyon
Sweetheart					Devil's Garden
Gang					29 Palms
Wife	Hubby				Joshua Tree Park
Girls	Boys				Palms to Pines Highway
Old Kid					Hidden Spring Canyon
HOW ARE YOU?					I'M STAYING AT THE
I AM					
Fine	Happy				I Danced at
Lonesome					I Dined at
Sad	Broke				WILL BE
Flying High					Seeing You
Enjoying the Desert					Away a Little Longer
WISH I HAD					Thinking of You
You	A Letter				Writing You Again
More Ambition	Lots of Handsome Men	Sun-bathing	In the Moonlight		Hitting the Hay
Someone to Love Me		Swimming	On the Desert		Stepping Out
More Sleep	The Desert Sunset	Golfing	On the Araby Trail		YOURS
THINGS ARE	Desert Wildflowers	Celebrating	To Andreas Canyon		'Till the Cows Come Home
Wonderful	The Canyons	Playing Tennis			With Love
Lovely	DOING LOTS OF	Bicycle Riding	To Seven Palms		Forever
Exciting	Sightseeing	I RODE HORSEBACK			Sincerely
I HAVE SEEN	Loafing	To Palm Canyon	I DROVE TO		NAME
The Mountains	Sleeping	On the Skyline Trail	Palm Canyon		
The Desert	Hiking		Date Gardens		
Lots of Pretty Girls					

Lazy Person's Correspondence Card   9A-H1172

STREET SCENE AT PALM SPRINGS, CALIF.

37

The Desert's Gambling Dens

THE DUNES
PALM SPRINGS
CALIFORNIA

Dinner Menu

The role of illegal gambling clubs in establishing Palm Springs' early reputation as a winter resort is often overlooked. Starting in 1931 with the construction of the Dunes Club in Cathedral City—an unincorporated area just east of Palm Springs—the Coachella Valley became known as one of America's prime gambling meccas prior to the dominance of Las Vegas after World War II.

The Dunes Club, hidden behind tall trees, was located just outside of Palm Springs' city limits.

The sprawling Spanish Colonial Revival–style Dunes Club was owned by Al and Lou Wertheimer of Detroit's "Purple Gang." However, to avoid the wrath of local churches and busybodies, the Wertheimer brothers barred Palm Springs residents from the club's gaming tables. Yet because of its plush dining room and cocktail lounge, the Dunes Club became a popular location for numerous Palm Springs society events, such as charity fashion shows "attended by the many socially prominent folk at the desert resort" in the 1930s, according to a *Los Angeles Times* article from the period.

Wise guys at the Dunes Club in 1940. Seated left to right: Phil McGraw, Leo Fields, Al Wertheimer, George "The Greek" Zouganiles, Joe Todaro, George Goldie, Samy Mykonos, "Doc" Kane, Nola Hahn, Joe Nelper, Art Sachse. Standing left to right: Harry Weiss, Chef Pierre, Albert the maître d', Hymie Portnoy, Dave Harris, Joe Hendricks. BELOW: 139 Club.

Another popular illegal desert gambling den—the 139 Club—opened in 1933 in Cathedral City under the ownership of the jovial Earl T. Sausser. More informal and much smaller than the nearby Dunes, the 139 Club was as well known for its famous chili recipe as for its gaming tables. To add to its outlaw allure, Sausser erected a squat lookout tower adjacent to the 139 Club's entrance that featured a prominent slit through which a machine gun barrel could emerge if required. He also hired large, dangerous-looking doormen who would admit patrons to the club only after scrutinizing them through a tiny peephole.

The third illicit gambling joint to cater to the Palm Springs crowd was the Cove Club, opened in 1941 by Jake Katelman and Frank Portnoy in Cathedral City, right on the border of Palm Springs near Highway 111. The building is currently the home of the Elks Lodge. Cove Club owner Jake Katelman would later migrate to Las Vegas, becoming the owner of the El Rancho Resort and Casino, after it became clear that business opportunities in wide-open Nevada were far greater than in Palm Springs, where dodging the law soon became tiresome.

All of the illegal gambling clubs were subject to intermittent disruption by Riverside County sheriff Carl Rayburn, who sent his deputies to break up the casinos in well-publicized raids. In 1936, the *Los Angeles Times* reported, "Sheriff's officers raided the swanky [Dunes] gambling club which is patronized by wealthy visitors to Palm Springs. Special investigators, posing as wealthy sportsmen, mingled with the guests until the signal was given for the raid when they assertedly [sic] confiscated costly gambling equipment as evidence." Such raids were mainly for show, however, as Sheriff Rayburn was kept well-juiced by Wertheimer and the desert's other gaming operators.

With the continuing success of the Dunes Club, Al Wertheimer (sans his brother, Lou) erected his own hotel in 1937—the Colonial House in Palm Springs—to accommodate some of the weekend gamblers his club was attracting.

In its basement, the Colonial House contained a small gaming room decorated with a risqué mural of naked women sporting 1930s hairstyles. After World War II, the Colonial House was sold to Bob Howard, who renamed it Howard Manor, turning its supper club into a popular Palm Springs hot spot.

Some weekend gamblers stayed at Al Wertheimer's Colonial House Hotel in Palm Springs.

Fire destroyed the palatial Dunes Club in 1943, whereupon Al Wertheimer opened the Dunes Restaurant on Palm Canyon Drive, which later became Ruby's Dunes after Wertheimer died in 1953.

The 139 Club appears to have closed in 1947, and the Cove ceased operations in the early 1960s.

Longtime residents, such as former mayor Frank Bogert, confirm that it was the presence of illegal gambling that attracted many Hollywood celebrities and wealthy industrialists with a weakness for the roulette wheel to Palm Springs, filling its hotel rooms, restaurants, and nightclubs through the nation's economic ups and downs.

The Dunes Restaurant was a popular nightspot.

A NATURAL COLOR REPRODUCTION FROM KODACHROME

8B-H523

At the Swimming Pool, the Tennis Club, Palm Springs, California

The Postwar Tourist Boom

PALM SPRINGS
on the Southern California Desert
AMERICA'S FOREMOST DESERT RESORT

Welcome!

THE IDEAL CONVENTION CITY

Suddenly, after World War II, it seemed that everyone wanted to visit Palm Springs. America's postwar prosperity allowed the middle class to discover what the rich and famous had known for years: Palm Springs was America's Foremost Desert Resort.

LEFT: The Tennis Club's oval swimming pool became world famous.

The western theme continued to be popular, as shown in places such as the Deep Well Guest Ranch and the exclusive Smoke Tree Ranch, both located in the south end of Palm Springs where Highway 111 heads east toward Indio.

Deed restrictions at Smoke Tree Ranch enacted in the 1930s limited homes to single stories, with undeveloped open spaces mandated between properties.

Smoke Tree Ranch encompassed a large area at the south end of Palm Springs. Today the ranch contains more dwellings within its original boundaries.

Smoke Tree Ranch was a prestigious—and very private—compound for industrialists and other blue bloods.

For tourists, the Old West could be experienced at popular chuck wagon breakfasts held out in the open desert a short ride from local hotels.

RIGHT: After World War II, open desert spaces started to disappear. In 1948, the shores of Tahquitz Creek were cleared for Palm Springs' first tract development, Tahquitz River Estates. BELOW AND FACING: Communal chuck wagon breakfasts were very popular with the tourists, who wore their cowboy fashions well into the 1960s.

Chuck-Wagon Meal near Palm Springs

K4376

Nineteen forty-seven was a big year for the Palm Springs tourist industry. Pearl McManus's fashionable Tennis Club, with its famous oval-shaped swimming pool, was enhanced with a new restaurant designed by the important Los Angeles–based architects A. Quincy Jones and Paul R. Williams. The same architects would go on to design the Town & Country Center three years later.

A stylized Tennis Club menu from the early 1950s.

Architect William Cody.

Also in 1947, the remarkable Del Marcos Hotel was completed. This was the first project designed by architect William F. Cody, and it received numerous awards for its innovative design.

Cody was a hugely talented force of nature, whose boisterous personality made him a legend in the Coachella Valley from his arrival in 1947 until his premature death in 1978. He was responsible for designing several of the most distinctive buildings in Southern California, including the Del Marcos Hotel, Huddle Springs restaurant, the J. B. Shamel and Abernathy residences, St. Theresa's Catholic Church, and the clubhouses of the Tamarisk, Thunderbird, and Eldorado country clubs.

ARCOS, Palm Springs, Cal.

William Cody's Del Marcos Hotel of 1947: *a tour de force* of Desert Modern design.

The Rossmore (right), the E. Stewart Williams–designed Bisonte Lodge (below), and the Lazy Lodge (facing below). All three have since been demolished.

Bisonte Lodge
PALM SPRINGS, CALIF.

the Warm Sands
of Palm Springs, California

LAZY LODGE

LAZY LODGE

ABOVE: The Warm Sands Inn, with its modest bungalows and small pool, was typical of the hotels in the south end of Palm Springs.

53

Southern California's Glamorous Desert Playground!

PALM SPRINGS
It's The
BONAIRE VILLAGE
BUNGALOWS

Open ALL Year

2675 North Indian Avenue
Palm Springs, California
Telephone: FAirview 4-1501

ABOVE: The Bonaire Village—in Southern California's Glamorous Desert Playground—was open all year. Telephone FAirview 4-1501 for reservations. Also note: artists' conception of typical Bonaire bungalow. RIGHT AND FACING BELOW: The lobby and double room of the high-style Desert Retreat.

ABOVE LEFT: The Del Hai Mo (huh?) Lodge. ABOVE: The Del Pico Lodge featured scary zombie-like guests relaxing poolside.

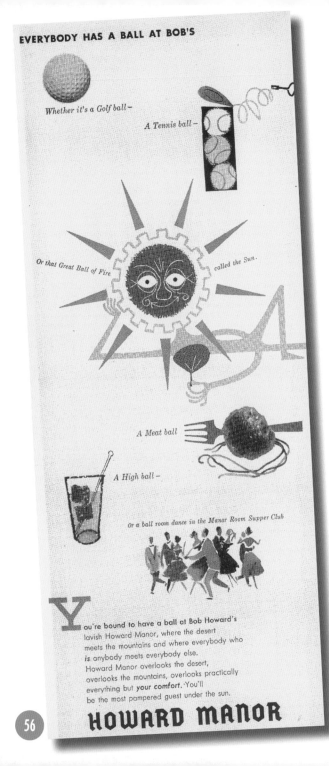

56

LEFT: Get into the swing of things with this hep ad for the Howard Manor; ABOVE: The Desert Riviera was one of many small hotels by prolific local designer Herbert W. Burns.

The oasis of La Paz Guest Ranch.

In 1948, Samuel Levin's stylish Biltmore Hotel appeared just south of the Deep Well Guest Ranch on East Palm Canyon Drive. With its swanky postwar styling by architects Fred Monhoff and Hank Gogerty, generous pool area, comfortable bungalows, golf course, dining room, and nightclub, the Biltmore had it all.

alcove suites with their luxurious sunken marble b rustic stone fireplaces . . . all tastefully and individ furnished. Your room has its own patio and indivi controlled refrigerated air and electric heating to provide you with perfect temperature control du both warm days and cool, restful nights.

Enjoy the ultimate in fine living . . . our sunken marble baths are a unique Biltmore feature.

At the right is the living room of your bed alcove suite . . . the real definition of luxury

The Biltmore's bungalows featured a sunken terrazzo tub that was fun for one in the '50s . . . for two in the sexy '70s . . . and for one again in the Reagan-era '80s.

The Biltmore's Dining Room.

The El Mirador received a major face-lift in 1952 by the famous African American architect-to-the-stars Paul R. Williams, who had done similar work for the Beverly Hills Hotel and L.A.'s Ambassador Hotel a few years

The El Mirador awash in pink to match the Beverly Hills Hotel's recent face-lift.

earlier. In 1954, Paul R. Williams would design Lucy and Desi's famous Thunderbird Country Club home. Eventually the El Mirador was absorbed into the Hilton chain before it was razed for the new Desert Hospital in the 1980s.

A typical *Palm Springs Villager* ad for the El Mirador.

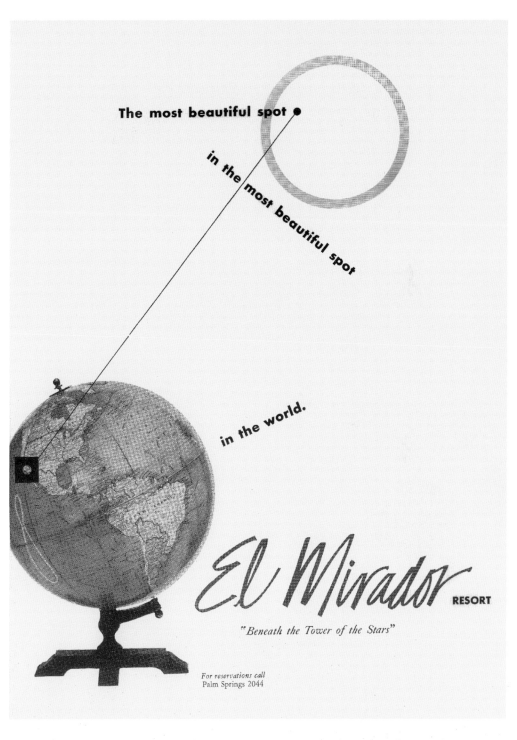

The most beautiful spot

in the most beautiful spot

in the world.

El Mirador RESORT

"Beneath the Tower of the Stars"

For reservations call
Palm Springs 2044

Your Own Slice of Paradise

Without question, in addition to tourism, speculative real estate has been the backbone of the growth of Palm Springs since the earliest white settlers and pioneers.

Realtors such as Culver Nichols, Harold Hicks, Tony Burke, and many others were colorful characters who helped sustain the Coachella Valley's real estate boom for many decades.

Others, such as Terry Ray, opened ultramodern realty offices that symbolized the exciting contemporary designs of second homes being constructed in the desert.

Culver Nichols, in his trademark 1954
Kaiser Darrin Roadster, was certainly
the most stylish of the local realtors.

Along South Palm Canyon Drive, Palm Springs, California

9B-H659

Shopping!

Part of the appeal of Palm Springs was its distinctive upscale shops arrayed along both sides of Palm Canyon Drive.

RIGHT: The famous Bullock's department store of Los Angeles established a branch location in Palm Springs in the late 1930s; FACING: Looking south on Palm Canyon Drive in 1949. La Plaza is on the left and Bullock's is on the right.

Bullock's Palm Springs, Palm Springs, California

Across South Palm Canyon Drive

Toward Bullock's Palm Springs, California. Tahquitz Canyon in the Distance

8B-H184

ABOVE: In 1948, Bullock's opened its posh new Palm Springs store across the street from the popular La Plaza shopping center.

RIGHT: In 1958, Robinson's jewel box of a department store opened on South Palm Canyon Drive.

Gabor clan matriarch Jolie Gabor operated her own glamorous boutique in the 1960s.

Palm Springs, California

Jolie Gabor

Waltah Clarke, Southern California's impresario of Hawaiian wear, not only had a home in Palm Springs but a branch of his clothing empire as well.

ABOVE: This 1960 postcard notes, "Waltah features 'round da clock' sportswear and cocktail wear. Also muu muus, sarongs, matching family swimwear, luau costumes, and accessories."; LEFT: Waltah Clarke relaxes with his lovely family.

CLARKE'S HAWAIIAN SHOP

Regular Waltah Clarke customers Judy and Bill Snow enjoy cooking thick steaks poolside—and had a postcard made to prove it. They're "having fun in the sun" at 1147 Paseo de Marcia in Palm Springs.

Town & Country Center

The Town & Country Center (highlighted with arrow) turned its back on the low-income properties of the tribe's Section 14.

A puzzling element of the Town & Country's design was that its east-facing side turned its back on Indian Avenue rather than embracing the street with large picture windows. The reason for this becomes clear when viewing historic aerial photographs from the time of the center's construction. Situated across from the property on the east side of Indian Avenue was Section 14, a one-square-mile parcel located in the center of Palm Springs that was the most prominent piece of the local Indian tribe's every-other-square-mile checkerboard reservation. This was the longtime home of many of the city's low-income residents and people of color, including many tribal members. As a result, city leaders considered Section 14 a visual blight, and businesses such as the Town & Country Center avoided facing the tribal property.

Designed by renowned master architects A. Quincy Jones and Paul R. Williams, the Town & Country Center was a mixed-use development of ground-floor retail shops and offices, second-story apartments, and the upscale Town & Country Restaurant.

It wasn't until 1959, following the Secretary of the Interior's decision to remove restrictions on long-term leases, that the tribe's Section 14 property began to receive new investment. One of the first to take advantage of the opportunity was developer Sam Benowit, who erected the upscale Spa Hotel on the northeast corner of Tahquitz Avenue and Indian Avenue in 1960. A few years later, a controversial decision by the tribe and the city to clear Section 14's remaining "slums" for new development resulted in the displacement of hundreds of residents and the destruction of its many buildings. The sorry episode remains a dark spot in the mid-century history of Palm Springs.

174 No. Palm Canyon – "Top of The Center"
Palm Springs, Cal.
Phone: FAirview 4-9906

PALM SPRINGS
TOWN & COUNTRY
RESTAURANT

The Palm Springs Girls always appeared in this formation as they wandered through the village in 1956.

The Palm Springs Hotel Explosion

A map from 1952 shows just how popular Palm Springs had become as a tourist mecca. Hotels, lodges, and small inns had sprouted like desert wildflowers all along Palm Canyon Drive, Indian Avenue, and many nearby streets.

FACING: In the early 1950s, Palm Springs was thick with hotels.

The San Jacinto Mountains proved one of
the world's most spectacular backdrops.

All sorts of accommodations, from trailer and mobile-home parks to mom-and-pop hotels, welcomed guests of every budget. Note that in Palm Springs the term "motel" was never used. Palm Springs was too classy to have motels but apparently not too classy to have trailer parks.

Neon signs were also banned in Palm Springs as being too garish. Instead, modest rear-lit plastic pole signs appeared—a few of which, due to their timeless understated appearance, front hostelries to this day.

In the 1950s, architect E. Stewart Williams added a cluster of modern buildings to the Pepper Tree Inn.

Shed roofs protected trailers from the blazing sun.

BELOW: Clearly not the bikini crowd, these gals are nonetheless joyfully soaking up the rays at the long-vanished Skylark Hotel. Notice the giant diving board, a once ubiquitous hotel feature that liability insurance has now rendered extinct.

RIGHT: Wearing a dazzling new bathing suit, this perky young lass strikes a modest pose at the Town & Desert Hotel as the family proudly looks on.

The Lido offered "Hospitality as Warm as the Sun."

Effervescent Mrs. Elnita Miller stands guard at Casa Elnita.

CONTINENTAL HOTEL, PALM SPRINGS

LUXURIOUS APARTMENT, POOLSIDE

LEFT: At the Continental Hotel, "ideally located" at 1380 North Indian Avenue, owner Lynne Jennings invites you to relax in the subdued surroundings of the hotel's guestrooms; BELOW: This is Gay's Mar-Roy Manor, a name that would prove more prophetic in the twenty-first century than the owners probably realized back in 1958.

Gay's Mar-Roy MANOR

ABOVE: The modern Park Lane was on the north end of town; BELOW LEFT: The Avalon Hotel featured a starburst architectural theme; BELOW RIGHT: Felice and Louis Thomas were your hosts at the Versailles Hotel and Apartments on Camino Monte Vista. Telephone FAirview 5–6248.

CLOCKWISE FROM ABOVE: Decades before the Mirage Resort's volcano extravaganza in Las Vegas, there was the same spectacle at La Fonda; Five gals and a T-Bird ornament the Brentwood "Deluxe" furnished apartments and hotel; At the Azure Sky Hotel and Apartments, guests enjoy refrigerated air-conditioning, TV and hi-fi in all rooms, and private patios for relaxed reading. Many of the units had kitchenettes; Finally, welcome to the no-frills Safari Villa.

SAFARI VILLA

PRIVATE PATIO

The Hotel Trinidad was known for its Purple Room, a restaurant/nightclub owned by this man, who represents everything that the author aspires to upon his retirement in this desert paradise.

Luxury FOR LESS

at Palm Springs' Newest and Most Unique Resort Hotel

The Palm Springs SANDS Hotel is located on 18 acres of beautifully landscaped grounds, secluded and private, yet right in the heart of town. It is impressively backdropped by one of the world's sheerest and boldest mountain escarpments at the site of the spectacular Aerial Tramway. With its breathtaking design, and its exotic lighting the Palm Springs SANDS conveys the feeling of enchantment.

This, combined with ultra modern facilities which have been provided for your comfort and pleasure, makes the Palm Springs SANDS the place to stay.

"We at the Palm Springs Sands hotel believe that all too often in the hustle-bustle of the world today, that the intended purpose of gracious inn-keeping has been sadly neglected and in some instances forgotten altogether. Here amidst the many splendored wonders of this fabulous desert and even more fabulous city, we hope to recapture the hospitality of the bygone era and make the Palm Springs Sands a place you will long remember—a place where you were welcomed not for your money alone, but for the friendship which we gained as a result of your being our guest. We would feel that we have failed miserably unless you left the Palm Springs Sands with the feeling that this is the place to which you would like to return often."

Today's Musicland Hotel was originally called the Casa Blanca.

A case study in middlebrow accommodations is the Monkey Tree. While the hotel's exterior architectural form is intriguing, the tastefulness of its interior décor is questionable. Today the property is a nudist resort where standing too close to the flames might prove hazardous.

The Holiday Inn became the Gene Autry Hotel, then Merv Griffin's Givenchy, and finally morphed into today's ultrahip Parker Palm Springs, proving that Palm Springs truly is the face-lift capital of the desert.

The Tropics was a Ken Kimes–built motor hotel. The Congo Room steakhouse was not tropical but African themed, although exotic enough for most people not to notice the incongruity. Like most cocktail lounges of the time, the Tropics' Cellar offered nightly dancing, except Sunday.

Part of the fantasy world of the postwar years was an attraction to a mythical Polynesia of balmy nights and free-spirited island gals, as reflected in tiki-themed hotels, restaurants, and bars. Although located in the desert, Palm Springs embraced Polynesia in places such as the Tropics Hotel, with its huge swimming pool ringed by carved tikis, thatched huts, and tropical landscaping.

The Ocotillo Lodge opened in 1956. It was erected by father-and-son developers George and Robert Alexander, who would later be identified with the Modern tract homes designed by architect William Krisel that they built throughout Palm Springs. By 1965, Palm Springs' housing stock had more than doubled, in large part due to the thousands of Alexander homes constructed by the firm over the preceding decade.

The Ocotillo, with its big pie-shaped pool, was owned by cowboy star Gene Autry for a short while.

Twin Palms Estates was the first Alexander tract development in the Coachella Valley.

Not coincidentally, the Alexanders, who were Jewish, chose to build their first housing tract—Twin Palms Estates—in the south end of Palm Springs. That was because up to that time, much of the city had been effectively rendered off-limits to Jewish ownership, due to restrictive covenants and de facto segregation. Similarly, many of the old established resorts such as the Desert Inn and the Oasis Hotel refused to accept Jewish guests. As a result, the mostly undeveloped south end of Palm

Springs (with the notable exception of the Waspy Smoke Tree Ranch) came to be associated with Jewish visitors, many of whom stayed at Jewish hotelier Samuel Levin's luxurious Palm Springs Biltmore that had opened in 1948. Change came quickly in the early 1960s, however, when the Alexanders' new tract homes built near the Racquet Club and adjacent to the city's tony Las Palmas neighborhood welcomed all buyers, regardless of race or creed.

Racial restrictions had also kept Jews from memberships in Palm Springs' Tennis Club and elite "down valley" country clubs such as Thunderbird in Rancho Mirage and Eldorado in Indian Wells. Which was why, in 1952, the Tamarisk Country Club in Rancho Mirage was founded so that Jews—particularly those in the entertainment industry—could have their own luxury golf facility in the desert. A decade later, Palm Springs' new Canyon Country Club would serve the same purpose.

Yet the city's Waspish old guard didn't seem to mind that their hotels were kept full in no small part because the Chi Chi—Palm Springs' largest, most fabulous nightclub— was owned by Irwin Schuman and his brother, who were Jewish.

The Twin Palms tract can be seen on the other side of Highway 111. The Biltmore Hotel with its bungalows is in the foreground.

The Canyon Club and Hotel, popular when built in the mid-1960s, was closed and disposed of in the 1990s.

The Schuman brothers were also responsible for opening the enormous Riviera Resort Hotel in 1959, where much of the 1963 Connie Stevens/Robert Conrad teen movie *Palm Springs Weekend* was shot.

At one time, the Riviera had its own nine-hole golf course.

Palm Springs Riviera Hotel / Beautiful 9 Hole Golf Course

Packing them in at the Riviera's cocktail lounge.

Don the Beachcomber president Sunny Sund sits in the Queen's Chair, surrounded by her friends.

Desert Dining

In addition to restaurants in hotels and nightclubs, Palm Springs presented a wide array of dining options, from the ordinary to the exotic.

On the exotic end was the Palm Springs branch of Don the Beachcomber's restaurant chain, which opened in 1953. Don offered potent rum-based tropical drinks, such as his signature Zombie cocktail, in an atmosphere resplendent with tropical décor and exotic music. At Don's, Oriental waiters served Cantonese food refashioned as delicacies from the South Pacific.

Cirone's Bit of Italy was a lovely Italian restaurant that moved across the street in the mid-1960s to become Banducci's Bit of Italy.

RIGHT: The short-lived Cirone's.

BELOW: Mama Banducci greets her guests in 1968 with menu in hand.

Banducci's, with its piano bar, was one of the last old-time Palm Springs restaurant and lounge combinations when it closed in 2004. Lyon's English Grille just down the street from the former Banducci's remains one of the best examples of mid-century dining and entertainment in Palm Springs.

AMERICA'S FINEST BARBECUED CHICKEN AND RIBS

Rudy's

PALM SPRINGS NEWEST, MOST UNIQUE RESTAURANT

1180 SOUTH PALM CANYON DRIVE

LEFT: Rudy's Bar-B-Q served a chicken dinner that was its "pride and joy." Now that's good eatin'.

Sips 'n Snacks advertised "the second best food in town . . . Mother's is first best."

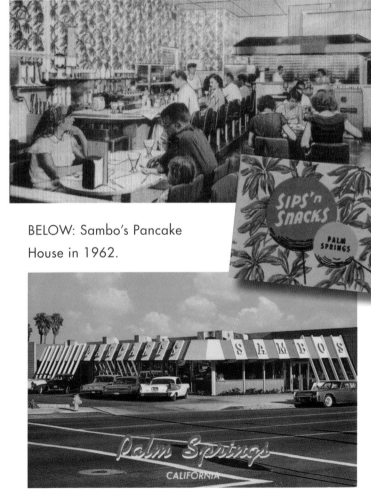

BELOW: Sambo's Pancake House in 1962.

In 1962, Chicago steak man George Diamond built the short-lived George Diamond Hotel and Steak House opposite the Racquet Club.

George Diamond shows off one of the four-inch steaks he's about to toss onto his charcoal broiler.

The Swiss Chalet with its Pumpernickel Room apparently got lost on its way to the Alps.

ABOVE: Mmmm, a mouthwatering spread at La Petite Marmite. BELOW: Paul D'Amico's '70s modern exterior and matador modern interior.

The famous topless Tahitian, Hina Ripa, appeared on the Chi Chi's menu covers, matchbooks, and other promotional materials.

The Chi Chi and The Doll House

In Palm Springs lore, it's the Chi Chi that longtime residents and visitors claim to miss most. Entrepreneur Irwin Schuman opened the Chi Chi Bar and Grill in 1936 and continued to expand the property until he sold it in the 1960s.

The Chi Chi's scandalous menu cover was originally painted on black velvet by artist Edgar Leeteg in the early 1940s while living in Tahiti. However, he received no credit for it at the time, commenting bitterly in correspondence to a friend, "No, of course I did not give Chi Chi permission to use my Hina Ripa to reproduce in any way. The least they could do would be to give me a credit line, but that is too much to expect from a Hollywood gin mill."

The changing face of the Chi Chi. Clockwise from above: These two gunslingers are headin' to the Chi Chi's Blue Room in the 1930s; The joint during the 1940s; In the early 1950s, the Chi Chi already took up a large part of the block fronting the Desert Inn; In 1957, local architect Howard Lapham transformed the Chi Chi into this space-age masterpiece, complete with starburst light fixture suspended over the driveway.

The BLUE ROO[M]

The expansive Chi Chi was divided into various dining areas and lounges to suit every budget and appetite. There was the elegant Blue Room, the Starlite Lounge, the smaller Chi Chi Lounge, the Grill Room, and also patio dining.

The Blue Room certainly had a lot of red in it.

Chi-Chi
PALM SPRINGS
CALIFORNIA

SOPHIA TUCKER

LENA HORNE

EDGAR BERGEN

DOROTHY DANDRIDGE

JERRY LEWIS

FIRST CLASS
POSTAGE
9 CENTS

EARTHA KITT

LOUIS ARMSTRONG

FRANKIE LAINE

LIBERACE

NAT "KING" COLE

Showplace of the Stars

JOSE GRECO

But it was the Starlite Room that was the shining monument to Irwin Schuman's vision and the magnet for attracting some of America's biggest stars to its stage.

Orchestra leader Bill Alexander welcomed stars such as Louis Armstrong, Nat "King" Cole, Liberace, Eartha Kitt, Edgar Bergen, and Jerry Lewis. The Palm Springs "Showplace of the Stars" also hosted Bob Hope, Jack Benny, Rosemary Clooney, and Sammy Davis Jr. during its heyday.

It's difficult to imagine today, but there was once a time in America—a bright and shining moment between the Great Depression and the late 1960s—when adults in cities throughout the country went to nightclubs to dine, hear a singer backed by a good band, dance, and stay up past midnight. This was a time when ordinary Americans in their forties, fifties, sixties, and older enjoyed a midnight supper during the Chi Chi's *second* show, ordering Welsh Rarebit or barbecued spareribs, and going to bed at 3:00 a.m. These days, only twentysomethings have the stamina to be out past 10 p.m.

Chi Chi

Chi Chi Lounge

Grill Room

Patio

Surroundings of
luxurious elegance
for Luncheon,
Dinner and Supper

Choicest Foods
expertly prepared

Open daily
11 a.m. to 2 a.m.

Dorothy Dandridge

Another of the beloved restaurant-nightclubs was the Doll House. Operated by the husband-and-wife team of George and Ethel Strebe from 1946 until 1960, the Doll House was phenomenally popular as an after-hours nightspot. Famous for its steaks and "icebox cake," people enjoyed dancing to the Guadalajara Boys until its 2:00 a.m. closing time.

ABOVE: Local artist O.E.L. "Bud" Graves created this clever ad for the back cover of the *Palm Springs Villager*. Welcoming you at the door are owners Ethel and George Strebe; RIGHT: A table tent from the 1950s.

Desert Modern

Palm Springs Villager

DESERT WILDFLOWER MAP AND PICTURES - In This Issue

Coachella Valley Savings and Loan #2 was designed in 1956 by E. Stewart Williams. It is especially compelling at night as it floats above Palm Canyon Drive.

Three architectural styles define mid-century Palm Springs: Rustic Ranch, Spanish Colonial Revival, and Desert Modern. All are equally valid and all coexist beautifully here in the desert. But it is Desert Modern—inspired by the sunshine, mountains, and desert sands of the Coachella Valley—for which Palm Springs has become internationally recognized in the twenty-first century.

Notable for its use of glass, deep overhangs, and indoor/outdoor spaces, Desert Modern embraces mountain views and the warm Palm Springs climate, defining a lifestyle of elegant informality.

Some of the best examples of Desert Modern architecture can be found in Palm Springs' collection of banks and former savings and loans located on South Palm Canyon Drive, many of which were designed by master architect E. Stewart Williams.

Williams was responsible for the International Style Santa Fe Federal Savings of 1957.

In 1960, Coachella Valley Savings moved down the street to its new Williams-designed headquarters.

Inspired by a visit to Le Corbusier's Chapel of Nôtre Dame du Haut in Ronchamp, France, architect Rudy Baumfeld of Los Angeles' Victor Gruen Associates paid homage to the master with his design for Palm Springs' City National Bank of 1959.

The reverse of the postcard notes the "Colorful view at dusk of one of several ultra-modern new banks, typical of the spectacular modern design of countless new buildings and homes springing up in America's Foremost Desert Resort."

"Typical" Bank in Palm Springs

CITY
National
BANK

City National Bank's ultra-modern design, both in concept and execution, was considered cutting-edge for its time.

SAFE DEPOSIT

One of the most important architectural statements along Indian Canyon Drive is the entrance canopy to the Spa Hotel, which is located on the site of the Indians' original bathhouse.

This ultramodern version erected in 1959 was called "the most beautiful bathhouse in the world"

when it was completed. Although the reflecting pond, sculpture, and glazed tile wall are long gone, the entrance canopy remains as a remarkable stylistic achievement.

Those worshiping in Palm Springs could attend William Cody's sculptural masterpiece, the St. Theresa Catholic Church. Built in 1968, its soaring interior and natural wood surfaces inspire contemplation.

Perhaps the most architecturally expressive restaurant ever designed in the desert was Huddle Springs by William Cody in 1957.

THE SPRINGS

A symphony of angles hovering over desert landscaping, the building was a sculptural masterpiece of wood, rock, glass, and metal. It later became the home of Aloha Jhoe's and Sherman's Deli and Bakery prior to being summarily razed in the early 1990s for a hotel that never materialized.

Palm Springs Aerial Tramway

As early as the 1930s, an aerial tramway connecting Palm Springs's magnificent Chino Canyon with the alpine heights of Mount San Jacinto had been envisioned by engineer Francis F. Crocker. It wasn't until 1963, however, that Crocker's dream would be realized.

Immediately upon its opening, the Palm Springs Aerial Tramway become one of the Coachella Valley's most popular tourist attractions. The lower tramway station was designed by local architects Albert Frey and John Porter Clark starting in 1950, thirteen years before its completion in 1963.

MOUNTAIN STATION
ELEV. 8,516'

Palm Springs
Aerial Tramway
Stairway to the Stars

VALLEY STATION
ELEV. 2,643'

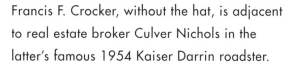

Francis F. Crocker, without the hat, is adjacent to real estate broker Culver Nichols in the latter's famous 1954 Kaiser Darrin roadster.

The lower tramway station is actually a bridge straddling a dry stream that can become a raging river during rainstorms.

Palm Springs Villager

FEBRUARY 1950

35¢

o. l. l. graves

THE SPECTACULAR TRAMWAY PROJECT . . . In This Issue

Ride the Palm Springs Aerial Tramway

The lower tramway station once boasted a small zoo, a snow arena with a stage, grandstand seating for 450 spectators, and—hard to imagine today—a dolphin pool in the desert.

The upper tramway is an E. Stewart Williams design evocative of a mountain chalet, dominated by a spacious dining room.

WINTER PLAYGROUND AREA

(map illustration)

PINTO BASIN

COTTONWOOD SPRINGS

TO DESERT CENTER AND BLYTHE.

BOX CANYON RD.

PAINTED CANYON — 195

MECCA HILLS

HIDDEN SPRINGS

CANAL

ECCA

DATE PALM BEACH
DESERT BEACH

BOMBAY BEACH

OASIS

SALTON SEA

FISH SPR.
SALTON SEA BEACH — 99

ERTINE ROCK

SEAVIEW BEACH

Going Down Valley

Until the late 1950s, the great swath of sparsely populated desert situated between Palm Springs and Indio, which some now call "down valley," was still referred to by many as "Palm Springs," both to avoid confusion for tourists and also to capitalize on the cache of the Palm Springs name.

At this point in our Palm Springs Holiday, let's put on our sunwear and rent a stylish new Hertz automobile so that we can motor on down the highway to the other communities that make up the Coachella Valley: Cathedral City, Rancho Mirage, Palm Desert, Indian Wells, La Quinta, Indio, the Salton Sea, and Desert Hot Springs.

100 PALMS

Cathedral City

ABOVE: Just over the border from Palm Springs on Highway 111 in Cathedral City was Laurye's Steak Ranch, a mid-century dinner house serving only the finest Midwestern corn-fed beef steaks and chops.

BELOW: At Walt Holman's Trailer and Marine Supply Company, you could combine the purchase of a desert house trailer with a new motorboat in one easy monthly payment. That's Walt out front at high noon.

Rancho Mirage

Farther down the highway, in what later became the city of Rancho Mirage, is the Desert Braemar cooperative housing development, completed in 1957. A colorful oasis in the desert, this speculative real estate venture would today be known as a condominium complex.

At the Desert Braemar, these cowgirls are being rudely ignored by the poolside residents. The original Desert Braemar still exists today.

The legendary Palm Springs cowboy mayor Frank Bogert managed many of the desert's dude ranches and topflight resorts, starting in the 1930s.

Thunderbird Country Club

Clockwise from above: In the late 1940s, Frank Bogert was the proprietor of the Thunderbird dude ranch in Rancho Mirage. Is that Mae West lounging poolside? In 1950, Bogert's dude ranch became the exclusive Thunderbird Country Club, which included the world's first golf course featuring homes nestled amongst the fairways; Motorized golf carts were invented at Thunderbird; During the day, Bogert's guests would take to the saddle in the open desert. By night, these same cowfolk would be on the dance floor at the Chi Chi, dressed to the nines.

AUTOETTE
Golfmobile
PUTS THE "GO" IN GOLF

Crosby, who periodically entertained his celebrity pals at the clubhouse of "America's most luxurious trailer park." Blue Skies is still as well kept and luxurious today, even with the passing of Der Bingle.

*T*wo years after the inauguration of the Thunderbird Country Club, the posh Tamarisk Country Club opened nearby.

Less sophisticated but still a class act was the Blue Skies Trailer Village, located just west of Thunderbird. Master planned by architect William Cody and beautifully landscaped, Blue Skies was developed by crooner and real estate mogul Bing

Blue Skies
TRAILER VILLAGE
Bing Crosby
PRESIDENT

AMERICA'S
MOST LUXURIOUS TRAILER PARK

Adjacent to Blue Skies Trailer Village was the since-vanished Palm Springs TraveLodge mobile home park, where the neighbors gathered for an informal gabfest.

One of the last dude ranches to survive in the area before new development rolled through was the famous White Sun Guest Ranch. In addition to horseback riding, guest ranch activities included swimming, pitch and putt golf, tennis, badminton, bike riding, and a children's play corral.

Desert Air

On the opposite end of Rancho Mirage, bordering the new community of Palm Desert, was the Desert Air hotel and airpark, where guests could "fly in or drive in" for a weekend getaway. One of the greatest expressions of postwar recreational freedom before the suffocating advent of security restrictions and other bureaucratic obstacles, the Desert Air invited pilots to fly their own planes to a desert resort where you could "taxi right up to your cottage."

Established by architect/proprietor Hank Gogerty and managed by his nephew Dan Callahan, the Desert Air survived until 1968. Situated on three hundred acres, the hotel's promotional brochure noted, "Occasionally the purr of an approaching airplane will announce the arrival of an air-minded guest. You'll watch the plane glide down to a landing on one of the green turf landing strips."

The Desert Air in the mid-1950s.

"Twilight brings its own special magic to the Desert Air. You'll meet a friendly and congenial crowd for cocktails in the Luau Hut and in the new Compass Room; after a delicious dinner there is informal dancing and entertainment; moonlight rides and picnics . . . lots of other special events at the hotel and in the community to add to the pleasure of your desert holiday."

ABOVE: View facing the pool; FACING: The Compass Room.

at mr. Gogerty's Hotel

The Luau Hut Bar at the Desert Air.
FACING: Relaxing in a bungalow.

7th ANNUAL DESERT AIR

Hawaiian Luau

Nº 497

SATURDAY, MAY 23, 1959

TARIFF: $12.50 PER PERSON

Includes Tahitian Rum Punch — 7 to 8 p.m.
The Feast — starting at 8 o'clock, followed by native
Hawaiian Entertainment. (includes all taxes and tip)

DESERT AIR HOTEL

Palm Desert Airpark • Palm Springs, Calif.

During the 1950s and 1960s, the resort's festive annual luau—with special guest stars such as Hilo Hattie—attracted over a thousand guests. A full Hawaiian feast and a bottomless tiki mug of rum drinks was only $12.75.

LEFT: Hotel manager Dan Callahan and his son Dan Callahan Jr.; RIGHT: Proprietor Hank Gogerty and Hilo Hattie (standing, center) during a Hawaiian prayer.

Up to a thousand people attended the Desert Air luaus in the late 1950s.

"Take this plate while I finish my drink."

Doin' the hula at the Desert Air.

Palm Desert

After World War II, entrepreneur Cliff Henderson envisioned Palm Desert, situated eleven miles east of Palm Springs, as the latest rival for the title of "America's Foremost Desert Resort."

Henderson claimed that Palm Desert's greater distance from Mount San Jacinto provided "Hours more sun—Lots more fun" during the winter season, in contrast to Palm Springs, where the sun went behind the mountain before 4 p.m. To take advantage of this extra-sunny clime, the Shadow Mountain Club was developed in 1948 by Cliff Henderson as a stylish new resort soon known for its distinctive figure-eight swimming pool.

The Shadow Mountain Club's famous figure-eight swimming pool. ABOVE: Cliff Henderson and friend at his new club.

Swimming Pool at Shadow Mountain Club, Palm Desert, California   8B-H525

PALM DESERT, CALIFORNIA
CLOSE COVER BEFORE STRIKING

Check out that wall fountain.

SANS SOUCI ROOM

In the mid-1950s, a joint venture between tire magnate Leonard Firestone and Cliff Henderson resulted in the construction of the Firecliff Lodge, located next door to the Shadow Mountain Club. With its space-age modern interiors, the hotel and restaurant was an ultrastylish escape from the desert sun. Sadly, the Firecliff Lodge no longer exists.

SPACIOUS LOBBY AND FIREPLACE

Fireplace as sculpture.

Along Highway 10, a billboard promotes Palm Desert in the 1950s. LEFT: Hal Kapp and Ted Smith serve up their slice of the desert; BELOW: Their graphically coordinated billboards.

DESI ARNAZ

invites you to his new WESTERN HILLS HOTEL where you may enjoy relaxation, sunshine and comfort in the finest accommodations on the desert, with every activity available including golf on the adjacent 18 hole Indian Wells Golf Course.

The charming dining room with its large picture windows affords a spectacular view of the pool, golf course and mountains.

Spacious studio rooms with most elegant decor have television, private lanai and cocktail bar.

Indian Wells

Farther east, in Indian Wells, television star Desi Arnaz inaugurated his new Western Hills Hotel in 1958, which was built right on the edge of the Indian Wells Golf Course. Later, the resort's name was changed to the Indian Wells Hotel.

BELOW RIGHT: Up a notch in class from the Indian Wells Country Club, the Eldorado Country Club was perhaps the most exclusive address in the desert for many years. This 1962 photo shows the William Cody–designed clubhouse dubbed the "Taj Mahal of golf" by its members; BELOW: Like most desert resort hotels of the time, Desi's hotel featured a popular cocktail lounge with stage backdrop for nightly entertaining and dancing.

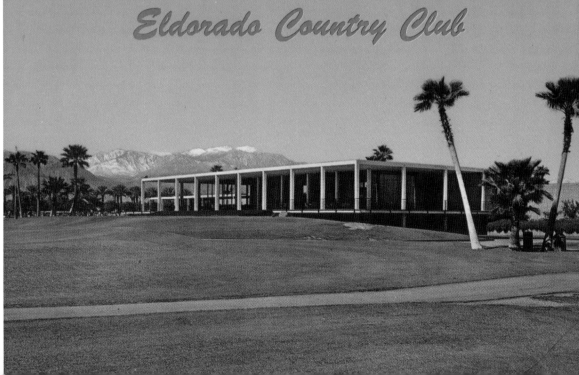

Another Indian Wells landmark was the Erawan Garden Hotel, erected circa 1960. The Erawan, with its Cambodia Dining Room and Moongate Lounge, was "completely oriental in both architecture and décor." Inspired by a Thai legend, the Erawan continued the tradition of transporting an exotic locale to the desert, just as the Tropics did with its Polynesian-themed resort in Palm Springs.

ERAWAN GARDEN HOTEL

All guest rooms have a magnificent view of beautiful Oriental Gardens, the desert, or the majestic Santa Rosa mountains. Rooms are spacious and luxuriously appointed, combining an original blend of Oriental beauty with modern convenience and comfort.

All rooms have radio, television and individually-controlled refrigerated air-conditioning.

The picturesque Kyoto bridge divides the swimming pool into two distinct areas — one for children and one for adults. Spend the whole day near the water if you like — sumptuous buffets served at the pool — one of the many added features which make a stay at Erawan so pleasant.

G

La Quinta

East of Indian Wells, the 1927 La Quinta Resort vies with Palm Springs for the title of having the first golf course in the Coachella Valley.

At La Quinta's Desert Club, "where winter never comes," both the European and American Plans were featured for pampered guests.

Continuing down
Highway 111 past La
Quinta we find the
Date Empire of Indio.

SNIFF'S BACK YARD

Indio

Starting in the late 1910s, Indio pioneers Floyd and Bess Shields, the Sniff family, and others imported date palms from North Africa as they established a date fruit industry in the desert. Due to the Coachella Valley's blazing summer heat and then-abundant supply of groundwater, it wasn't long before Indio became the date capital of America, providing over 90 percent of the country's date crop.

LEFT TO RIGHT: In his backyard, Mr. Sniff, along with his two dogs, inspects a crop of luscious dates; Since 1953, at Shields Date Garden and Showroom, the slideshow "The Romance and Sex Life of the Date" has run in a continuous loop in its theater; Floyd Shields stands proudly next to the "Mother Tree"—imported from Algiers—and three generations of her family.

LEFT: Wrapping the maturing dates in paper keeps rainwater from spoiling the fruit; ABOVE: A typical roadside date stand in the 1930s; BELOW: The distinctive Garden of Eden on the Indio–Palm Springs Highway.

Cheerfully hand-sorting
those luscious dates.

In addition to dates, the Coachella Valley became noted for its bountiful citrus crops.

LEFT: These are perhaps the largest grapefruit ever grown—although there is something slightly naughty about this photograph.

As Indio's fame grew during the 1930s, it not only became a day-trip destination for Palm Springs tourists but a holiday destination in its own right.

LEFT: Pruning a date palm in the 1920s; BELOW: Other accommodations embraced the Spanish theme, such as Indio's Rancho Las Adelfas Guest Cottages.

RANCHO LAS ADELFAS GUEST COTTAGE
Indio, Cal.

ABOVE: The Hundred Palms Resort, with its tourist cabins, was a typical Indio lodging; BELOW LEFT: Indio's small downtown also boasted the two-story Hotel Indio, with its sixty-three steam-heated rooms where you could luxuriate in "the land of dates, desert flowers, and bright sunshine." BELOW RIGHT: After World War II, newer accommodations appeared, including Indio's version of the Biltmore Hotel, designed by Herbert W. Burns of Palm Springs.

The Indio Date Festival began in the early 1920s as a celebration of the annual date harvest. Given the origin of Indio's date palms, it seemed appropriate that the festival's theme would be Baghdad and the Arabian Nights, although in recent years those names conjure up decidedly less romantic images than in the past.

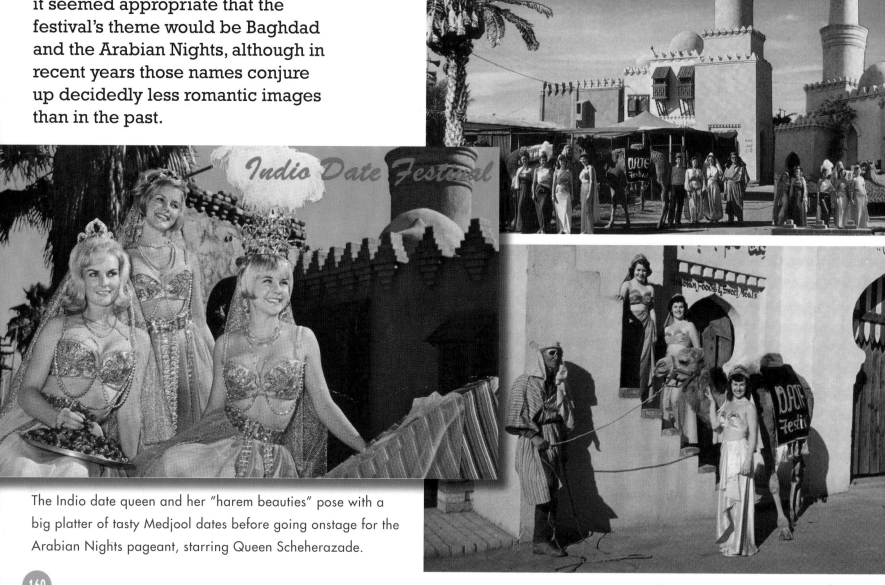

The Indio date queen and her "harem beauties" pose with a big platter of tasty Medjool dates before going onstage for the Arabian Nights pageant, starring Queen Scheherazade.

The Sultan and his harem at the 1963 Indio Date Festival.

Hanging out in Indio.

Salton Sea

As we motor through Indio toward the far eastern end of the Coachella Valley, we encounter the Salton Sea. This giant, visually arresting inland lake was created when the Colorado River was accidentally diverted into the dry lakebed for two years starting in 1906. The Southern Pacific Railroad constructed a bridge across the sea's wide expanse on its route to Los Angeles.

The moonlit Salton Sea.

The Southern Pacific's *Sunset Limited* crosses the Salton Sea on its way to Los Angeles in the 1920s.

Speedboat racing on the Salton Sea
was popular in the 1940s.

Hell's Kitchen on the Salton Sea's romantic Mullet Island in 1943.

Sunset on Salton Sea
250 ft. below sea level
Coachella Valley, Calif.

ABOVE: The dramatic topography surrounding the Salton Sea inspired art photography and recreational activities for many decades.

BELOW: In the 1950s, boat races, waterskiing, and fishing were especially popular at the Salton Sea.

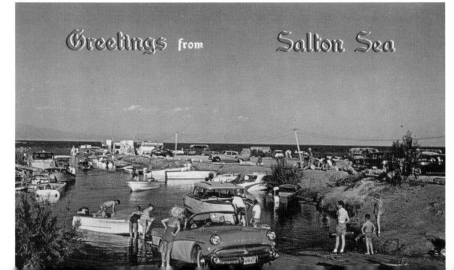

Greetings from Salton Sea

Greetings from Salton Sea

Salton Riviera

In the late 1950s, aggressive developers attempted to package the Salton Sea as a fabulous investment opportunity for the general public. Among a handful of hucksters, Azusa-based M. Penn Phillips was the most brazen. In 1958, he created the Salton Riviera development and marketed the Salton Sea as the world's largest, most luxurious playground.

Your dreams come true in...

SALTON RIVIERA

California's fabulous new resort city on the Salton Sea

The great visionary: M. Penn Phillips.

Salton Riviera
AND SALTON SEA

California's "American Mediterranean" is a pleasant 45 minute drive from Palm Springs. You arrive in a wonderland of exciting, refreshing water sports... fishing to satisfy every Isaak Walton... a wealth of duck hunting... or just plain relaxing in the refreshingly balmy breeze of an inland sea. Salton Riviera may well become California's largest completely planned all-year resort community. Beautiful 80 foot frontage homesites to Spacious 3 acre estates, should make the Salton Riviera a 2000 home community within the next three years. The M. Penn Phillips Company, world's largest land development and home building company, expects Salton Riviera's development costs for engineering, streets, water, marinas, airports, etc. to exceed $20,000,000

According to Phillips, the Salton Riviera combined "the excitement and beauty of Capri, Monaco and Bermuda," with Hawaii thrown in for good measure. He set up huge tents on the property and bused folks in from the Los Angeles area, creating a buyer's frenzy with live music, celebrity performances, and free food and drink.

M. Penn Phillips's Salton Riviera development.

SALTON RIVIERA

California's fabulo[us] resort city o[n] Salton S[ea]

M. Penn Phillips's modern new sales office inspired confidence in eager investors, who soon had purchased most of the Salton Riviera's available lots.

Then, in 1960, M. Penn Phillips suddenly announced his retirement and sold the whole operation to another company. What caused his hasty departure? Did he have a premonition of the toxic trifecta of high salinity, algae blooms, and massive fish die-offs that would soon tarnish the Salton Sea's reputation? Or had he decided that it was time to just cash out? Regardless, it wasn't long before the sea's noxious smell would smother the real estate boom. In addition, catastrophic flooding destroyed many beachside structures, including the Salton Bay Yacht Club and the North Shore Yacht Club, constructed on opposite sides of the sea.

ABOVE: Salton Bay Yacht Club rendering; FAR RIGHT: The 1964 Salton Bay Yacht Club's interior; RIGHT: The Salton Sea's Desert Garden motel.

North Shore Yacht Club

Entrepreneur and oilman Ray Ryan—owner of the El Mirador Hotel and father of Bermuda Dunes—decided that North Shore Beach was the "glamour capital of the Salton Sea." In 1958, Ryan retained Palm Springs architect Albert Frey to design the nautically inspired North Shore Yacht Club. Utilizing his trademark materials of sand-colored concrete block, corrugated steel, yellow fiberglass panels, and porthole windows, Frey created a Modern masterpiece in the eastern Coachella Valley.

North Shore Beach
Glamour Capitol of Salton S

ABOVE: Architect Albert Frey's nautically inspired North Shore Yacht Club is on the left; RIGHT: Ray Ryan's North Shore Yacht Club, harbor, and adjacent motel.

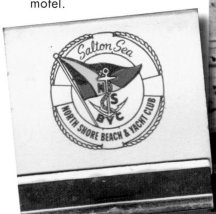

Desert Hot Springs

From the Salton Sea, our Palm Springs Holiday takes us northwest along old Highway 99 through Thermal, Coachella, and Thousand Palms Village to Desert Hot Springs, known as "the finest health spa in America," according to the city's Rental Owners Association.

Although hot springs were discovered in the area in the 1920s, it wasn't until 1941 and the arrival of L. W. Coffee's Hot Mineral Baths that the gold rush of small mom-and-pop spa motels—or Spa-Tels—began appearing throughout the Desert Hot Springs hot water zone.

L. W. Coffee's Hot Mineral Baths was Desert Hot Springs' first Spa-Tel.

Catering primarily to the working class and the occasional spa-crazed European, Desert Hot Springs offered a relaxing getaway for those who didn't mind crowds.

Stylin' at the Tradewinds.

Another Spa-Tel glamour shot.

Throw in a few potatoes and carrots and soup's on!

At the Tropical Spa-Tel, kiddies in kimonos were always welcome.

Clockwise from above: At the opposite extreme, you could sit virtually alone amongst the minimalist landscaping of the Lido Palms; In the 1990s, Miracle Manor became a trendy getaway spot; Something seems amiss with the color of the pool water at the Little Admiral Inn Spa-Tel. Perhaps they piped in the water from the Salton Sea.

Now *this* is an appealing motel!

An aerial view of the Healing Waters Trailer Village,
circa 1960, with its par 3 golf course, shows how
easily the desert was tamed by visionary men.

At the Desert Hot Springs Cabot's Lodge, folk artist Cabot Yerxa built his interpretation of a New Mexico–style Indian pueblo as a tourist attraction.

Greetings from Desert Hot Springs

As our sojourn comes to a close and we pack our suitcases for the journey home, our hearts gladden at the thought of returning next season for a Palm Springs Holiday in America's Foremost Desert Resort.

Peter Moruzzi is the author of *Havana Before Castro: When Cuba Was a Tropical Playground*. An architectural historian, Moruzzi is an expert on mid-century Modern architecture and design. He is the founding president of the Palm Springs Modern Committee and resides in the Silver Lake District of Los Angeles and in Palm Springs.

Palm Springs Villager

o. e. l. graves

50c

DESERT WILDFLOWER MAP AND PICTURES • In This Issue

C-16